T0321845

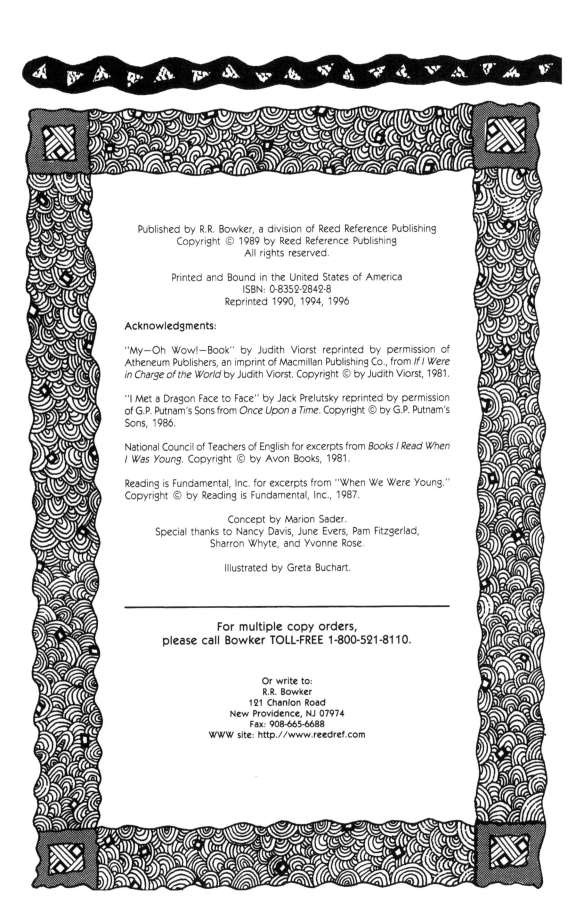

Printed and Bound in the United States of America
ISBN: 0-8352-2842-8
Reprinted 1990, 1994, 1996

Acknowledgments:

"My—Oh Wow!—Book" by Judith Viorst reprinted by permission of Atheneum Publishers, an imprint of Macmillan Publishing Co., from *If I Were in Charge of the World* by Judith Viorst. Copyright © by Judith Viorst, 1981.

"I Met a Dragon Face to Face" by Jack Prelutsky reprinted by permission of G.P. Putnam's Sons from *Once Upon a Time*. Copyright © by G.P. Putnam's Sons, 1986.

National Council of Teachers of English for excerpts from *Books I Read When I Was Young*. Copyright © by Avon Books, 1981.

Reading is Fundamental, Inc. for excerpts from "When We Were Young." Copyright © by Reading is Fundamental, Inc., 1987.

Concept by Marion Sader.
Special thanks to Nancy Davis, June Evers, Pam Fitzgerlad, Sharron Whyte, and Yvonne Rose.

Illustrated by Greta Buchart.

**For multiple copy orders,
please call Bowker TOLL-FREE 1-800-521-8110.**

Or write to:
R.R. Bowker
121 Chanlon Road
New Providence, NJ 07974
Fax: 908-665-6688
WWW site: http://www.reedref.com

The Private And Personal Reading Journal

This journal is your very own personal record of books you have read. Whenever you finish a book, write in the title, the Author, the dates, and your thoughts and feelings about the book. When you have filled its pages, this journal will be about you and your Reading — from beginning to end— Have FUN!

The first book I remember reading was _____

_____

I like to read books that _____

_____

The best book I have ever read is _____

_____

My favorite author is _____

_____

My favorite character in a book is _____

_____

I wish there were more books written about _____

_____

My Private And Personal Reading Journal's
TABLE OF Contents

Here you can list all the books you have described in your journal. Then, whenever you want, use the Table of Contents to find your favorites again!

My—Oh Wow!—Book

I'm lying here
and I'm sick in bed
with a terrible
horrible
pain in my head,
and these funny bumps
that my ma says look
like the chicken pox,
and my—oh wow!—book,
and some Band-Aids (six)
for the spots I hurt
where I fell on stones
when I missed the dirt,
and my—oh wow!—book,
and my swollen thumb
that the door slammed on,
and this aching stom-
ach from fifths on root beer
and thirds on pie,
and my—oh wow!—book,
which I'm not gonna die
till I finish.

by
Judith Viorst

What book are you reading now?

Use this first page in your *Private and Personal Reading Journal* to write about that book. Describe your favorite characters, the story, what you like best and least, and anything else you especially want to remember. It's just for fun...and just for you!

Title _____

Author _____

Date Read _____

My Comments _____

_____

_____

_____

_____

_____

_____

_____

_____

_____

_____

_____

_____

_____

_____

_____

_____

Early books were written by hand on specially prepared animal skins called vellum.

Now I'm reading...

Title _____

Author _____

Date Read _____

My Comments _____

_____

_____

_____

_____

_____

_____

_____

_____

_____

_____

_____

_____

"A novel is a garden carried in the pocket."
-- Arabian proverb

6

My latest book is...

Title _____

Author _____

Date Read _____

My Comments _____

_____

_____

_____

_____

_____

_____

_____

_____

_____

_____

_____

_____

_____

_____

7

" There are more treasures in books than all the pirates' loot on Treasure Island... and best of all, you can enjoy these riches every day of your life."
-- Walt Disney (1901-1966)

Recommended Books

Look for these the next time you visit the library!

If mystery, adventure, and suspense give you a thrill, try
The True Confessions of Charlotte Doyle by Avi
The Haymeadow by Gary Paulsen
Weasel by Cynthia DeFelice
The Case of the Purloined Parrot by E. W. Hildick
The Twin in the Tavern by Barbara Brooks Wallace

If you love reading books that make you laugh, try
The Poof Point by Ellen Weiss and Mel Friedman
Your Mother Was a Neanderthal by Jon Scieszka
The Best School Year Ever by Barbara Robinson
Wayside School Is Falling Down by Louis Sachar
Attaboy, Sam by Lois Lowry
The Boys Start the War by Phyllis Reynolds Naylor

If animals books bring out the beast in you, try
Redwall by Brian Jacques
Martin's Mice by Dick King-Smith
Poppy by Avi
The Prince of the Pond by Donna Jo Napoli
Shiloh by Phyllis Reynolds Naylor

If you like getting to know kids from both the past and the present, try
Catherine, Called Birdy by Karen Cushman
Mayfield Crossing by Vaunda Micheaux Nelson
Class President by Johanna Hurwitz
Time for Andrew by Mary Downing Hahn
Monkey Island by Paula Fox
Maniac Magee by Jerry Spinelli
Yang the Youngest and His Terrible Ear by Lensey Namioka

If you think fantasy and science fiction books are out of this world, try
Shape Changer by Bill Brittain
Jennifer Murdley's Toad by Bruce Coville
The Daydreamer by Ian McEwan
Of Two Minds by Carol Matas and Perry Nodelman
The Giver by Lois Lowry

I just finished reading…

Title _____

Author _____

Date Read _____

My Comments _____

_____

_____

_____

_____

_____

_____

_____

_____

_____

_____

_____

_____

_____

_____

_____

_____

"A good book
is good company."
-- Henry Ward Beecher
(1813-1887)

I really liked reading this book...

Title _____

Author _____

Date Read _____

My Comments _____

_____

_____

_____

_____

_____

_____

_____

_____

_____

_____

_____

_____

_____

_____

_____

_____

Many years before there were books, the word "read" meant to figure out the meaning of puzzling events in nature. Reading is still magical today because it is the key to understanding the mysteries of the world we live in.

This time, I read…

Title _____

Author _____

Date Read _____

My Comments _____

_____

_____

_____

_____

_____

_____

_____

_____

_____

_____

_____

_____

_____

_____

_____

_____

_____

"The Time to read is anytime."
-- Holbrook Jackson
(1874-1948)

Books Remembered by World Class Readers

Some people you'll recognize recall wonderful books from their childhood...

Judy Blume, Children's author
Madeline by Ludwig Bemelmans and *Betsy-Tacy* books by Maud Hart Lovelace.

Bill Clinton, President of the United States
The Silver Chalice by Thomas Costain, *The Last of the Mohicans* by James Fenimore Cooper and *The Robe* by Lloyd C. Douglas.

Bill Cosby, Entertainer
The Bible, Aesop's Fables and *The Adventures of Huckleberry Finn* by Mark Twain.

Jacques Cousteau, Oceanographer, writer and film producer
The Jungle Book by Rudyard Kipling and *White Fang* by Jack London.

Billy Joel, Singer and composer
A Connecticut Yankee in King Arthur's Court by Mark Twain.

Ann Landers, Newspaper columnist
Charlotte's Web by E.B. White.

Sandra Day O'Connor, Justice, Supreme Court of the United States
Mary Poppins by Pamela L. Travers and *Winnie the Pooh* by A.A. Milne.

Charles M. Schulz, Cartoonist and creator of "Peanuts"
Sherlock Holmes by Sir Arthur Conan Doyle.

Willard Scott, TV Personality and *Today Show* weatherman
The Bible and *The Little Engine That Could* by Watty Piper.

Maurice Sendak, Author and illustrator of children's books
The Princess and the Goblin by George MacDonald.

Stephen Speilberg, Motion Picture Director/Producer
The Leatherstocking Saga by James Fenimore Cooper and *Treasure Island* by Robert Louis Stevenson.

Patrick Swayze, Actor
Tarzan of the Apes by Edgar Rice Burroughs.

Oprah Winfrey, TV Personality
Strawberry Girl by Lois Lenski, *A Tree Grows in Brooklyn* by Betty Smith, and *Clover* by Dori Sanders.

Here's another title
I'm adding to my journal…

Title _____

Author _____

Date Read _____

My Comments _____

_____

_____

_____

_____

_____

_____

_____

_____

_____

_____

_____

_____

_____

Lovers of libraries owe a special
thanks to Benjamin Franklin. In
1731, he established the first
subscription library in America.
He charged members fees and
used the money he received to buy
more books.

13

Here's another book
I want to remember...

Title _____

Author _____

Date Read _____

My Comments _____

_____

_____

_____

_____

_____

_____

_____

_____

_____

_____

_____

" Books are songs, musical flourishes, high notes, low sounds,
and lullabies -- so take your time, select a good book,
open your eyes, close your ears to the outside
noises... and come sing with me. "

--Anita Baker Bridgforth
(1958-)
Singer & entertainer

14

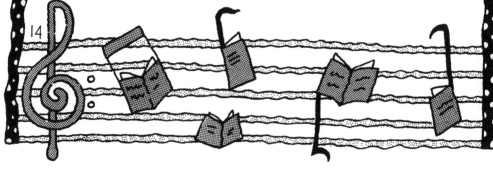

I would recommend this book to my friends…

Title _____

Author _____

Date Read _____

My Comments _____

_____

_____

_____

_____

_____

_____

_____

_____

_____

_____

_____

"There is no frigate
like a book
To take us Lands away…"
--Emily Dickinson
(1830-1886)

15

I'm finishing my journal by reading…

Title _____

Author _____

Date Read _____

My Comments _____

_____

_____

_____

_____

_____

_____

_____

_____

_____

_____

_____

_____

_____

In 1947, while searching for a stray goat in a cave a young peasant boy made an astounding literary discovery. Rolled in ancient clay jars were the Dead Sea Scrolls - the oldest known copies of The Bible and the world's rarest "books"

I Met a Dragon Face to Face

I met a dragon face to face
the year when I was ten,
I took a trip to outer space,
I braved a pirates' den,
I wrestled with a wicked troll,
and fought a great white shark,
I trailed a rabbit down a hole,
I hunted for a snark.

I stowed aboard a submarine,
I opened magic doors,
I traveled in a time machine,
and searched for dinosaurs,
I climbed atop a giant's head,
I found a pot of gold,
I did all this in books I read
when I was ten years old.

by Jack Prelutsky

9 780835 228428